A Celebration of the Millennium

Photography by **Michael Thompson and Miles Cowsill**

Text by **Stan Basnett**

Edited by **Trevor Barrett**

Designed by **Tracey Harding**

Published by **Lily Publications (IOM) Ltd**

PO Box 1 Portland House Station Road
Ballasalla Isle of Man IM99 1AB

Telephone **01624 823848**

ISBN **1 899602 16 X**

It was with much pleasure that I agreed to write the foreword to ***Spirit of Mann,*** *which is a refreshingly accurate and concise portrayal of the history of the Isle of Man.*

Historically the Island was dependent on agriculture, fishing and tourism. As these traditional industries declined, efforts have concentrated on building a balanced and diversified economy.

As well as being scenic and rural in character, the Island has a low crime rate, a clean environment, friendly people, plenty of space and a peaceful, slower pace of life, which is attractive to both old and new residents. A commitment to preserving this quality of life is central to our Government policy.

Looking back over the changes which the Island has gone through, I feel it is significant that all those elements that are important and contribute to the Manx way of life, which we cherish and enjoy, have been preserved. At the same time, the Isle of Man has been able to progress a combination of other unique and significant features to develop the Island into a thriving, well-regulated centre for reputable business, many of whom have supported this publication.

I am sure you will find ***Spirit of Mann*** *both enjoyable and interesting.*

Hon Donald J Gelling MHK
Chief Minister

AFD Software Ltd,
International Address Management Centre,
Old Post Office Lane, West Quay, Ramsey,
Isle of Man, IM8 1RF.
Telephone: (01624) 811711.

Bank of Bermuda (Isle of Man) Limited,
PO Box 34, 12/13 Hill Street, Douglas,
Isle of Man, IM99 1BW. Telephone: (01624) 637777.

BARCLAYS

Barclays Bank PLC,
PO Box No 135, Eagle Court, 25 Circular Road,
Douglas, Isle of Man, IM99 1WE. Telephone: (01624) 684444.

Barclays Private Bank & Trust (Isle of Man) Limited,
PO Box 48, 2nd Floor, Queen Victoria House, Victoria Street,
Douglas, Isle of Man, IM99 1DF. Telephone: (01624) 682828.

Shane Magee at 31 Victoria Street, Douglas,
Isle of Man, IM1 2SE.
Telephone: (01624) 623778. Fax: (01624) 623284.

Department of Tourism and Leisure,
Sea Terminal Buildings, Douglas, Isle of Man, IM1 2RG.
Telephone: (01624) 686801.

Halifax International (Isle of Man) Limited,
PO Box 30, 67 Strand Street, Douglas, Isle of Man, IM99 1TA.
Telephone: (01624) 612323. Fax (01624) 670086.

Isle of Man Bank, PO Box 13, 2 Athol Street, Douglas,
Isle of Man, IM99 1AN. Telephone: (01624) 637000.

Isle of Man Post Office, Philatelic Bureau,
PO Box 10M, Douglas, Isle of Man, IM99 1PB.
Telephone: (01624) 686130. Fax (01624) 686132.

LEXICON
BOOKSHOP
Est. 1936

63 Strand Street, Douglas, Isle of Man, IM1 2RL.
Telephone: (01624) 673004.

Manx Airlines Limited,
Ronaldsway Airport, Ballasalla, Isle of Man, IM9 2JE.
Telephone: (01624) 826000. Fax (01624) 826001.

manx
independent
carriers

Distribution Centre, Snugborough Trading Estate, Braddan,
Isle of Man, IM4 4LG. Telephone: (01624) 620185.

Queen Victoria House, 41-43 Victoria Street, Douglas,
Isle of Man, IM1 2LF.
Telephone: (01624) 633633.
www.manx-telecom.com

Isle of Man Steam Packet Company,
Imperial Buildings, Douglas, Isle of Man, IM12BY
Telephone: (01624) 645645. Fax (01624) 645609.

VALMET

Valmet Isle of Man Limited,
Valmet House, Summerhill Business Park, Victoria Road,
Douglas, Isle of Man, IM2 4RW.
Telephone: (01624) 631600. Fax: (01624) 677523.
E-mail: ValmetIOM@valmetgroup.com
Web: http://www.valmetgroup.com

Spirit of Mann

'Spirit of place' – any place – is the most difficult and elusive quality to capture in words, so I am indeed fortunate that the wonderful photographs of Michael Thompson and Miles Cowsill leave me with the relatively easy task of telling something of the history of the Isle of Man (known traditionally as Mann).

History tends to be thought of in terms of a series of dates and events. But this is a story of people: Mesolithic and Iron Age dwellers, pioneering preachers, conquering warlords, fearless seafarers and eminent Victorians. Each remarkable in their own way, as borne out by the legacies they have left behind.

And while it is the Island's history that sets it apart from the rest of the British Isles, there are countless other aspects of the Manx way of life which make a lasting and favourable impression on so many visitors. As reflected by the fact that over the years, a considerable number have chosen to become residents of the Island, and have never looked back.

Discovering the spirit of Mann has to be a personal and first-hand experience. We hope that this book will take you some way along the journey – and give you the impetus to complete it by setting foot on the Island at least once in your lifetime.

Stan Basnett

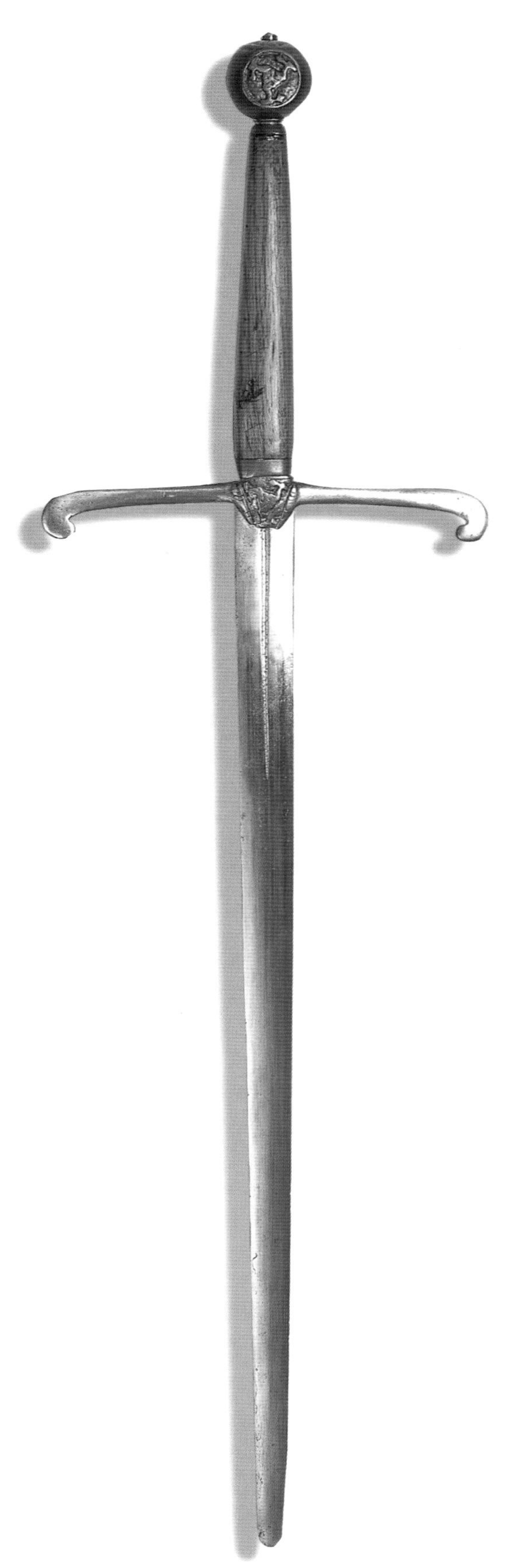

INFANT MANN

Part of the land mass that became the British Isles, Mann is composed of some of the world's oldest stratified rocks, formed as layer upon layer of mud and sand was deposited beneath the sea. The subsequent upheaval of this slate eventually formed the backbone of the Island.

The battle scars of its formation are to be seen in the Island's contrasting coastline. This varies between the limestone pavements and volcanic remnants in the south, the contorted slate strata of the east, the alluvial plain of the north, and the sand cliffs, sandstone and slate of the west. In the central area are a number of igneous granitic outcrops and accompanying metalliferous intrusions. Completing this dramatic sculpture are the rounded hills and deep glens cut by the advance and retreat of Ice Age glaciers. The result is a landscape to take the breath away – a geological gem set in an emerald sea.

The northern plain was created from debris dropped by the retreating ice sheet and the run-off from the uplands as the last remnants gradually melted. This meltwater, later named the Sulby River by the Norse, left large lakes throughout the flood plain as it made its way to the sea. In the process it also formed Sulby Glen, one of the largest and most beautiful glens in the Island.

At one time during the early upheaval, Mann was almost certainly connected to the rest of Britain by a land bridge. Great Deer – more popularly known as Irish Elk – roamed the Island in the latter stages of the Ice Age. Remains of these animals have been found near dried-up lakes, the most likely explanation for their demise being that the weight of their antlers caused them to overbalance while drinking and they subsequently drowned. Two complete skeletons have been preserved – one in the Manx Museum at Douglas and one in Edinburgh.

As for human habitation of Mann, the earliest clues discovered to date are standing stones and flint remains from the Mesolithic Age. Neolithic dwellers followed, in the period 4000 to 2000 BC, and there are many visible signs today of Bronze Age occupation from 2000 to 500 BC. Neolithic monuments, stone circles and long barrows can be seen at the Meayll or Mull Hill (meaning bare or bald hill) at Cregneash; Cashtal yn Ard (castle of the height) in Maughold; several sites in Lonan; and at other locations in the Island where modern names such as the Giant's Grave have hidden their true origins. The excellent Manx Museum in Douglas has a number of fascinating presentations to satisfy the more curious scholars of Mann's ancient history.

The Celts spread into Europe from about the sixth century BC. Indo-European people, they came to Britain from south-west Germany, bringing with them a culture still evident in Brittany, the Scottish Hebrides and Highlands, Wales, Cornwall and the Isle of Man. The earthwork remains of their great roundhouses on the Island can be seen today at Ballanorris (Norris's homestead), the Braaid (a gorge), and Ballakeighan (Mac Akoen's farm). There are also traces of Celtic promontory forts, often built on areas of previous occupation.

The Celts endowed the Island with traditions and folklore still remembered by many Manx folk. Perhaps the most famous is the legend of Manannan Mac Lir, the Celtic sea god who lived on the Island and was able to shroud it in mist to protect it from invasion by other deities.

Tradition has it that Christianity reached Mann from Ireland by St Patrick and his disciples. They established numerous keeills throughout the Island, the remains of which can be seen at numerous locations, none more dramatic than those at Lag ny Killey (hollow of the church) on the western coast below Cronk ny Arrey Laa (hill of the day watch). Many of the present churches in the Island are built on the site of these early keills, and many of the parish names are derived from the names of early saints.

Christianity was integrated into the Celtic way of life, the new preachings working alongside some of the pagan beliefs. Records of this period are preserved in Celtic crosses and on Ogham stones, and perhaps the most dramatic example of the melding of the two cultures can be found at Lonan Old Church, where a Celtic wheel-headed cross stands in a socket stone.

The Celts, whose period of occupation was one

The Neolithic chambered tomb at **Cashtal yn Ard**

Next page **North Barrule** ridge from **Snaefell**

of prosperity and peace, were farmers and tribal by nature, dividing land with treens and quarterlands – a form of land tenure which has largely survived to the present day. Quarterland boundaries can still be seen, marked by large white stones, the significance of which is gradually being lost. The way of life of these early settlers is now brilliantly portrayed in the House of Manannan – an exciting new heritage centre in Peel which is part of the Manx National Heritage Story of Mann.

The Romans also knew of the Island, referring to it as Mona – the same name they gave to Anglesey – but by AD 74 Pliny the Elder was calling it Monapia. A runic cross in Kirk Michael bears yet another name, Maun, and there are early Irish and Welsh references to Mannan and its Celtic derivatives. There is no positive evidence that the Romans ever settled on the Isle of Man, though they may well have set foot on it knowing it to be fertile and inhabited. Could it have been too wild and windswept for them?

Castle Rushen

The Vikings

Next to arrive on Mann were the Vikings. There is no doubt that the Norsemen came by sea, marauding in their great longboats, as was their stock in trade. They made landfall on the Island and claimed it for the King of Norway but, as with all their conquests, the Viking chieftains vied with each other for supremacy. They were remarkable seamen and saw Mann as strategically placed to mount their attacks on the surrounding islands. The Manx, however, resisted the Viking occupation, and it was only after several bloody battles that the Norse invaders could lay claim to the Island. In 1079 Godred Crovan landed at Ramsey in the north and attacked the Manx who, suffering many casualties, surrendered. The battle took place on the slopes of Scacafell or Sky Hill (its Norse name was Skógarfjall, meaning wooded hill) not far from the ancient landing place at the mouth of the Sulby river.

The Norsemen came to Mann by way of the Western Isles of Scotland, which were divided into the Nordreys (the northern group) and the Sudreys (southern group). The kingdom of Mann and the Isles included the Sudreys (or more correctly the Sudr-evjar), and the Vikings also had a presence in York and Dublin, at one time ruling the Isle of Man from the latter.

The Vikings were to have such a profound effect on Mann that much of their influence has survived to the present day. This includes Tynwald – the form of government they introduced after conquering the Manx and settling on the Island as permanent residents. The importance of Mann in Viking culture can be gauged by the fact that other than in their native country, it is only in the Island and Iceland that their spirit is perpetuated in common everyday forms of government and place names. The Vikings' practice was to assemble their freemen at a meeting field within their area every year at midsummer and proclaim the law (the so-called breast law) one to another. Such courts were known in Norse as the Thing. They survive in Mann as Tynwald (Thing-võllr the Parliament field) and in Iceland as the Althing (Al-thing the Parliament field). The Icelandic Parliament dates from 930, making it the oldest parliament in the world. The Manx Parliament originated in 1079 and still follows the principles laid down by the Viking settlers.

The Viking Kings of Mann eventually married into the Island community, following the tradition of previous inhabitants by building in areas which had been occupied before. They expanded earlier Celtic settlements and established fortifications

such as those on the fertile lowlands of the southern plain at the site of the present Castle Rushen and at Cronk Howe Mooar (a mixture of Norse and Gaelic meaning great mound hill). These fortifications took the form of earth mounds surmounted by a wooden palisade, and the remains of the latter can be seen behind a local authority housing estate near Port Erin. By the end of the Viking era, the mound at the site of Castle Rushen had developed into a stone tower.

In Viking days the northern plain was still covered with lakes, of which the three largest were Lake Mirescog (later derived to Lough Mallow, meaning swan plain lake), Lough Dhoo (the dark lake) and Loughan ny Yeiy (the pond of the geese). For many centuries these freshwater lakes were valued for their fishing and eventually became abbey lands. Half of the fishery of Lake Mirescog was granted to the Bishop of Mann and the Isles by Magnus, son of Olave, in 1257. In modern times the lakes have been drained to bring land into cultivation, but remnants of them still remain here and there and further proof of their existence survives in farm names such as Ellan Bane (white island) and Ellan Rhennie (island of bracken).

Christianity was already established on the Island before the Vikings arrived, having been introduced by wandering Irish saints and monks whose calling it was to spread the word. Although pagans, the Vikings tolerated the religion, and maybe it was this fusion of Celtic and Viking ways, mixed with early Christian beliefs, that set the Manx apart from the rest of the British Isles. Certainly, there is still a fierce independent spirit in the indigenous population who are without doubt proud to be Manx – and it doesn't take long for newcomers to fall under the Island's spell either .

Stan Basnett

Douglas Lifeboat carries the name of the founder of the **RNLI – Sir William Hillary**

The inner harbour at **Douglas**

Kings of Mann

The last Viking king was Magnus, who followed Ivor the Usurper in 1252. King Alexander II of Scotland had for a number of years been engaged in discussion with King Haakon of Norway for the surrender of the Hebrides to Scotland. In 1263 Haakon, joined by Magnus, King of Mann, fought at Largs in the Clyde to defend the Western Isles from the Scots but was defeated by the weather and in battle. With Norse power ended, King Haakon retreated to Kirkwall, Orkney, where he later died. Alexander allowed Magnus to return to Mann where he ruled until his death in 1265. Independence based on Norse rule ceased, and though there followed a period of struggle between the Scots and the English for sovereignty of the Island, the Viking influence was to prove indestructible.

Norse origins are evident in many of Mann's place names and family names, as well as in the formal legislature with its Keys, Deemsters, Coroners and Lockmen. The church too was formalised under Norse rule, but the language remained Celtic. The Vikings' occupation is also recorded in the remains of their longhouses, many of which are to be found on the sites of Neolithic and Celtic settlements. Other significant finds are a number of ship burial sites, particularly those at Knock y Doonee (hill of the church) in Andreas and at Balladoole (Doole's farm) in Arbory. Burial sites have also been excavated at Ballateare (Teare's farm) and Ballachrink (hill farm), both in Jurby, where Viking artefacts have revealed much about their way of life.

Without doubt the most significant finds have been at Peel Castle, where recent excavations have uncovered details of many centuries of settlement on St Patrick's Isle, on which the castle stands. The fortification of the isle (which was known to the Norse as Holmpatrick) was strategic from the Viking point of view, and several Kings of Mann lived here between 1098 and 1237, the last being Olaf II. A Norse grave discovered at Peel records one of the richest female burials outside of Scandinavia. Jewellery and cooking utensils were buried with the pagan woman to equip her for life in the next world!

For two hundred years following the death of Magnus, Mann's last Viking king, the islanders suffered as a result of the feuding between the Scots, English, Norse and even their Irish cousins for sovereignty of the Island. A final stand was made against the Scots by the Manx at Ronaldsway in 1275 in support of Godred, son of Magnus. The Scots emerged victorious from a battle in which Godred and many others were killed.

In 1405 control of the Island was given to Sir John Stanley on the condition that he presented two falcons to King Henry IV and that his family gave similar homage to all future kings of England at their coronation.

During this period the fortifications at Peel and Castletown were developed to their final state. Peel Castle in this form is generally attributed to William le Scrope, who was King of Mann between 1392 and 1399. Castle Rushen is even more interesting and is without doubt one of the best-preserved castles of its type in the British Isles. This can be attributed to its continued, albeit intermittent, use since the time of Magnus, and also to the fact that it is built in limestone, unlike the sandstone structure of Peel Castle.

Castle Rushen was rebuilt and expanded from the early Viking fortification by the Scots and the English. Most of its Norman architecture came from the period when William de Montacute held the kingship from 1333 to 1344. His son succeeded him and the castle was largely completed before the end of the 14th century.

The buildings within the curtain wall of Castle Rushen are still used to this day as a courthouse. The castle is also a major visitor attraction and a significant part of The Story of Mann, presented by Manx National Heritage.

Lords of Mann

From 1405 stability returned to Mann under the rule of the Stanleys, who were very close to the English royal household. The family relinquished the title of King of Mann, preferring to be 'a powerful lord rather than a petty king', and thus the title Lord of Mann was ascribed, and still exists. The present Queen is the Queen Lord of Mann.

By this time Castletown had become the capital of the Island and Castle Rushen the residence of the Lord. The Stanleys set about formalising the laws of the land which until their time were breast laws held in the stewardship of the Deemsters. In 1429, under the rule of Sir John Stanley, and while Henry Byron was Governor, the laws of the Island were set down in writing for the first time. Uniform weights and measures were also determined and at the same time the power of the church was reduced.

In 1627 James – Lord Strange, 7th Earl of Derby and a member of the House of Stanley – succeeded to the position of Lord of Mann. He was affectionately known by the Manx as 'Yn Stanlagh Mooar' (the Great Stanley) and his form of government was to have a lasting effect on the Island.

During the period of the English Civil War the Island escaped direct involvement but in 1651 saw a conflict of its own. The Lord was away fighting for the Royalist cause while the Countess stayed in residence at Castle Rushen and William Christian, the Lord's Receiver, was left to administer the Island's affairs. Instead he raised the Manx in rebellion against the Countess, joining forces with Colonel Duckenfield and the Commonwealth troops to lay siege to the castles at Peel and Castletown. Those Manx loyal to the Lord surrendered and the castles survived without the kind of damage that Cromwell was inflicting on many others. William Christian ('Illiam Dhone' – Brown William) eventually gave his life in the cause of freedom for the Manx after the Island was restored to the Stanleys in 1660. Three years later he was shot at Hango Hill for his part in the rebellion.

The return to Stanley rule led to a further period of stability. In 1698 Bishop Wilson was appointed by William, the 9th Earl of Derby, and he soon realised that the Island's most pressing problem was the tenure of real property, much the same as in Ireland. The policy of Godred Crovan since his victory at Sky Hill in 1079 had made the people mere tenants at will, but for many centuries there was more land to till than men to till it, leading to control of the movement of the people. Furthermore, no one was allowed to leave the Island without the express licence of the Lord. The tenancy was severe, the buildings poor and conditions barely tolerable, yet the tenant was required to deliver the Lord's rent! Little wonder that the rebellion of 1651 had its roots in the question of land tenure, which took the form of a copyhold or 'straw tenure'. The customary method of conveying land was by verbal agreement and the symbolic surrender of a straw by the grantor to the grantee.

For a long period before the bishop's arrival the Island had been in the stewardship of successive governors and the Lord was in effect an absent landlord. The Bishop, who was both an ecclesiastic and a statesman, was so distressed at what he found that he persuaded the Earl of Derby to come and see for himself. He did so in 1699, following which he instructed the Bishop to set about settling the land on the tenants. Earl William died before much progress was made. His brother, James Stanley, succeeded him as the 10th Earl of Derby and reluctantly maintained the policy. Consequently, in 1704, the Keys drew up their proposals for settlement, which dragged on until 1866.

James Stanley was the last of the Derby family, and when he died in 1736 the Isle of Man passed to the second Duke of Atholl. This new line ruled until 1765, subsequently becoming Governors of the Island from 1793 to 1830.

From Smuggling to Lifeboats

Laxey Wheel – Lady Isabella named after the then-Governor's wife Lady Isabella Hope

During this period of the Island's history, the lucrative occupation of smuggling developed. Perhaps it was fired by the long-running disputes over land tenure, but whatever the motivation many of the population earned considerable fortunes importing brandy, rum and silks to the Island, and eventually everyone got in on the act.

Independent from the rule of the British Parliament, Mann took full advantage of its unique position and framed its own laws, which did not impose heavy revenue dues on such imports. The Lord himself received a handsome income by applying only modest duties, and the Islanders made a very comfortable living from the 'import and export business', which was never seen as smuggling.

Many wealthy English and continental merchants were attracted to the Island and set up residence. Castletown and Douglas became the principal ports through which the business was conducted, with the Manx running cutters between the Island and various ports in Britain. Excellent seamen, they soon learned to evade the increased number of revenue cutters and coast watchers that the British Government had initiated in an effort to stop the trade. Some of these officials were not averse to doing a bit of illicit business on their own account, using small inlets such as Port Grenaugh and other places where caves provided a natural sanctuary. Tales from this colourful era still live on in the memories of many Manx families.

Inevitably, the British Parliament eventually decided that enough was enough, and attempted to bring the Duke to book. First they introduced the Mischief Act in 1765, giving revenue officers the right to stop and search every boat going in or out of any port, Manx or otherwise.

This led to the Revesting Act, which set about relieving the Lord of his manorial rights. The Duke sought compensation and Tynwald did not see that the Island should foot the bill – hardly surprising in view of the fact that at this time the House of Keys was self elected and the domain of the wealthy landowner. As part of the settlement the Duke of Atholl was appointed Governor of the Island, an arrangement felt by the people to be preferable to the period when the Island was briefly under the control of English officials.

The last of the Atholls to reside in the Island as Governor was John Murray. The 4th Duke of Atholl, he built Castle Mona as his official

Douglas harbour

residence in a commanding position in the centre of the sweep of Douglas Bay.

It was in the latter half of the 18th century that Methodism came to the Island thanks to a travelling preacher named John Crook. Methodist societies were initially established at Castletown and Peel. John Wesley visited Mann in May 1777, the year in which the first chapel was built in Peel. A second was built in Lonan in 1780. Methodism soon had a stronghold in the Island and chapels and reading rooms sprang up not only in the towns but in many remote communities.

The Island also attracted a number of foreign debtors who by seeking residence here were able to escape their creditors. It became such a problem that legislation was passed in 1814 to allow for prosecution for liabilities incurred elsewhere.

But the Isle of Man still appealed as a place to live to half-pay officers and others enticed by the low prices and tax benefits – and none more so than Sir William Hillary, who came to the Island in 1808 having lost a personal fortune raising the largest private army in England to fight for king and country against the French. Not only had the family coffers gone, but also money invested in foreign sugar. Living in a house that overlooked Douglas harbour, Hillary witnessed the horror of people perishing at sea as numerous vessels ran into difficulties trying to enter the harbour. It ultimately led him, in 1824, to establishing a National Institution for the Preservation of Life from Shipwreck – a body which later became The Royal National Lifeboat Institution.

At this time the Isle of Man's fishing industry was thriving, along with supporting boatbuilding yards, rope works and sail manufacturers. Many exported their products, and a particularly good market was Liverpool – a city with whom the Island and its seafarers forged strong and lasting links.

A touch of Victorian **Douglas**

The Industry of the Victorians

Victoria became Queen in 1837. Thus began an era of great industrial progress and the development of an architectural style reminiscent of medieval gothic. It was a time when many entrepreneurs enjoyed a bonanza to rival the gold rush of the Yukon. The stakes were high and fortunes were won and lost.

The Island owes much of its present fabric to this age, and particularly to prominent Victorians. People such as Major J S Goldie Taubman MHK for his persistence in promoting the steam railway; Thomas Lightfoot for the horse tramway; George William Dumbell, Alexander Bruce and Charles Nelson for promoting several tramways; Henry Bloom Noble for his benevolence to the town of Douglas; G H Wood for his diligent service to the Isle of Man Railway; Dalrymple Maitland, at one time owner of the Union Mills; William A Hutchinson, a director of the Isle of Man Bank and captain of the parish of Marown; and many others who left their indelible mark.

The subsequent appointment of Governors Hope and Loch was to prove of great benefit to the Island, as they positively encouraged the Manx in their disputes with the British Government. They belonged to the more enlightened Victorian age and during their time much change took place. The increase in the wealth and population of Douglas led to it becoming the capital of the Island during Governor Loch's period of office. Public health became an issue and legislation was put in place in 1860 to improve sanitation, provide water and generally improve living conditions. A determined effort was made on the improvement of streets and highways throughout the Island and attention given to furthering standards of education. The harbours had been neglected for many years and a start was made to improve them by carrying out repairs and building new breakwaters. There was work to be done and a period of frenzied activity started at a pace that had not been seen before.

Horse tram on **Douglas promenade**

Mining

Mining for lead and zinc was already well established in the Island but reached its zenith in this period of Mann's history. In the middle of the 19th century £80 shares in the Laxey Mining Company were selling at more than £1,000. No small wonder when you consider that by 1876 the annual value of lead, silver and copper ore shipped from Laxey reached more than £90,000, and its silver mines were the most productive in the British Isles.

Laxey was the industrial centre of the Island. Records of mining in the area date from 1781, but by the mid 1800's there were seven main shafts in the Laxey area. The deepest was Dumbell's shaft, which reached a depth of 302 fathoms (552 m), with interconnecting galleries extending almost 2 miles underground. The lower valley floor was taken up with the washing floors of the Great Laxey Mining Company. It was a massive undertaking.

The population of the village had increased significantly and, with public houses on the doorstep, the need for a place of worship within the village was long overdue.

It is not surprising that G W Dumbell was one of the Laxey Mining Company's principal shareholders. It was he who was instrumental in promoting a church to be built right in the middle of the village, on part of the garden of the house where the captain of the mines lived. The church was designed by Ewan Christian, a Manxman famous throughout Britain for his church architecture, and was built largely by the miners themselves. The foundation stone was laid in 1854 by the bishop, Lord Aukland. With due ceremony the church was consecrated on Tuesday 27th May 1856, the mines being closed for the day to allow those for whom it was built to participate.

1854 was to be a year to remember in Laxey. The mines were now so deep that flooding was a very real problem, and Robert Casement, a Manxman and engineer to the Great Laxey Mining Company, designed a large and elegant waterwheel to pump the water out. It was commissioned in 1854, amid much pomp and circumstance, by Lady Isabella Hope, the wife of the then-Governor of the Island. The wheel was duly named *Lady Isabella* and, at 22.5 metres in diameter, is still the world's largest waterwheel and a big attraction for today's visitors to Laxey.

The lower area of the mines is also open to the

public. It is part of The Story of Mann and is well worth seeing to gain an insight into the conditions under which miners worked, and to marvel at the sheer size of the wheel.

Other industries in the lower part of the Laxey Valley included St George's woollen mills, which were introduced by John Ruskin in 1881, and a power station housing the boilers and generator sets that provided electricity for the Laxey and East Coast Tramway, built in 1894. In 1860 Richard Rowe, captain of the mines, built a flour mill in the Glen Roy Valley where it joins the Laxey Valley. The two mills are still in use today.

Another major mining operation was the Foxdale lode. Located in the west of the Island, south of St John's, it was worked at the same time by a number of individual operators who in 1828 came under the control of The Isle of Man Mining Company. By the middle of the century there were three main shafts in use at Foxdale. The deepest was Beckwith's shaft, which had reached 320 fathoms (585 m) by 1855. Starting in slate it finished in granite and was known to be 'hot'! The workforce at Foxdale at this time was around three hundred and fifty, with many women and children working on the washing floors. In the last half of the century a total of 149,063 tons of lead and 50 tons of silver were won from the mines here – all by hand.

In 1886 the Foxdale Railway was built from Foxdale to St John's, where it connected with other railways to the rest of the Island. It not only carried the ore to Ramsey for export but also provided a regular passenger service.

The mining industry reached its peak at the end of the century but by 1911 had virtually ceased. The market for silver was effectively killed off when its value in silver coinage became more than the face value of the coin itself. The British Government responded by introducing the Coinage Act of 1920, allowing alloys to be used in the minting of coin.

Not for the first time there was an inevitable migration of labour from the Island. They abandoned their cottages and crofts and went to pastures new. Many of the miners and their families found their way to the United States and in particular to the Colorado area. The resourcefulness of the Manx, who can be found in all corners of the world, is intrinsic to the spirit of Mann.

The Birth of Tourism

A predilection of the Victorians was to 'take the waters' and English resorts such as Bath, Brighton and Eastbourne became very fashionable. The working classes were not to be outdone and places like Blackpool had also started to develop as landowners saw the potential. Here, streets were laid out and elegant houses built, followed by boarding houses in the wake of the arrival of the railway. Blackpool also had the first street tramway in Britain.

Not surprisingly, local businessmen and entrepreneurs from the north-west of England quickly realised the possibilities for this new industry in the Isle of Man. They set about the redevelopment of Douglas and the other principal towns on a scale which even yet has to be rivalled. Hundreds of boarding houses were built along with major hotels and places of entertainment. New roads were set out and Douglas expanded into new residential areas built on land formerly belonging to large private estates. Much of that fabric is only now being replaced as Douglas assumes a new mantle dictated by the growing needs of the finance sector.

By popular myth, Douglas takes its name from two rivers which join and flow out through the harbour around which the town developed. The River Glass (the grey river) rises in the West Baldwin on the side of Injebreck Mountain, and the River Dhoo (the dark river) rises on the slopes of Greeba Mountain and flows down the central valley.

In 1863 Douglas became the administrative capital of the Island, coincident with the appointment of Sir Henry Brougham Loch as Governor. It had grown since the time of the Atholls through the Regency period with grand town houses being built along Bucks Road, Finch Road and Derby Square on the outer edge of the town. There were villas and large residences along the fringe of the bay at the Villa Marina and at the Castle Mona, with Clarence Terrace and the Esplanade extending the town northwards. The rapid expansion which took place between 1870 and 1910 soon put Douglas ahead of Blackpool.

The whole of the Loch Promenade was reclaimed from the foreshore on a new alignment. In 1874 work started on the new sea wall to enclose the area, and three years later the wall and the

Manx Electric Railway at **Laxey Station**

new promenade were complete. The fine Victorian facade, much of which exists to this day, grew out of the development of the reclaimed land to provide boarding house accommodation for visitors, who were now flocking to the Island in their thousands. In 1872 the official figure was 60,000 visitors and by 1884 this had almost reached 183,000.

Upper Douglas was laid out with grand squares and gardens with terraces of fine houses, leaving a legacy which still forms the character of the town. In 1851 there were 1,193 houses in Douglas and in the next twenty-five years this figure had doubled. By comparison the Island's total population in 1851 was 52,387, yet a quarter of a century later it stood at 53,763.

The Transport Revolution

With the tourism industry came another revolution – transport. Although only a small island, Mann was at the forefront of new transport technology.

Communication between Whitehaven and the Isle of Man since 1767 had been by sailing cutter once a week. This was subject to the vagaries of the weather and occasions are recorded when a period of six weeks went by without any sailing from Whitehaven. From 1819 steamships called at the Island but their service was intermittent and less than satisfactory.

In 1829 a group of local businessmen met in Douglas under the chairmanship of High Bailiff James Quirk and formed the Mona's Isle Company to own and operate a shipping company. This was to be the forerunner of the present Isle of Man Steam Packet Company, which is one of the oldest shipping companies in the world. They took delivery of their first vessel, *Mona's Isle*, in 1830, just eighteen years after the invention of steam-powered ships. Their fourth vessel, *King Orry*, was built at John Winram's yard in Bath Place, Douglas, with engines supplied by Robert Napier. Launched in 1842, it was the largest and fastest vessel in the fleet, making the sailing to Liverpool in seven hours. It was the last wooden vessel to be built for the company and the only one constructed in the Island.

Road transport on Mann was limited to horse-drawn carriages, and in 1833 travel between Douglas and Castletown by the stage coach *William IV* was only available on alternate days and took two hours. On other days the coach ran to Peel and back and connected with a coach to Ramsey at Ballacraine. The Ballacraine Hotel sported hitching hooks for horses on its roadside walls, a feature which survived to the hotel's last days as a public house. By 1837 the coach *Beehive* was offering daily return travel between Douglas and Ramsey by way of Kirk Michael, leaving Douglas at 9.00 am and Ramsey at 4.00 pm. The journey time was four hours, although in winter it could take considerably longer.

It is hard to imagine just how difficult travelling conditions must have been in those days, but a perfect illustration is served up by the fire which occurred in January 1844 at King William's

College at Castletown. This was spotted by the night guard at Castle Rushen, and a detachment of the 6th (the King's) Liverpool Regiment was sent from the Castle Barracks to assist. At the same time a courier was despatched to Douglas to fetch the Sun Insurance Company's fire engine. Because of the wintry conditions and the state of the roads it took five hours for the engine to come from Douglas, a distance of just nine miles! It was time for change and, led by J S Goldie than an hour and from Douglas to Ramsey a little under ninety minutes.

At this time the Island even supported two separate railway companies – the Isle of Man Railway Company of 1873 and the Manx Northern Railway Company of 1879. Seven years later the Foxdale Railway was built, becoming the Island's third steam railway. By 1904 they were all absorbed into the Isle of Man Railway Company and came under its control.

Villa Marina Gardens in **Douglas**

Taubman MHK – later to become Speaker of the House of Keys – a group of local businessmen tried several times to attract investment in a steam railway to connect the Island's principal towns. Eventually, in 1873, the Isle of Man Railway Company became reality after a struggle with funding which was resolved with the help of the Duke of Sutherland and Sir John Pender, both of whom were leading railway financiers and directors of the London and North Western Railway. They saw the potential of building a narrow-gauge railway – a development which by 1879 had changed the Manx way of life and opened up travel for everyone on the Island. A journey from Douglas to Castletown took less

But that's not the end of the story – far from it. Thomas Lightfoot, a Sheffield contractor, came to the Island to retire but like so many before and since became restless. Seeing an opportunity within the emerging tourism business he promoted the idea of a tramway for Douglas Bay. As a result, work started on the Douglas Horse Tramway in 1876 to build a line the whole length of the promenade. It survives to this day, operating as a summer-only attraction, and still gives visitors a taste of what life was like for those holidaying Victorians who treated themselves to a leisurely ride along Douglas promenade on a tram drawn by a specially-bred horse.

The rapid expansion of Douglas was enough to fire the interest of a number of far-sighted local businessmen in a speculative development of part of the Howstrake Estate at the northern end of the bay, extending into Onchan. They decided to service this with roads and a new electric tramway. The necessary powers to enable them to do so were contained in the Howstrake Estate Act, with provision initially for the tramway to extend as far as Groudle.

The venture blossomed into the Isle of Man Tramways and Electric Power Company Ltd. and the route ran further north to embrace both Laxey and Ramsey. The travel time between Douglas and Ramsey was consequently reduced still further, and the tramway served a second major purpose – as a tourist attraction still not rivalled anywhere else in the British Isles.

The men who invested in the project had seen what was happening on the Fylde coast and, wanting some of the action, had been rewarded for their vision.

By 1894 the same promoters had acquired the horse tramway and had tried to extend their electric tramway south along the promenade at Douglas. The Corporation, opposed to the unsightly poles needed to supply power to the trams, rejected the proposal, even though there was the offer by the company to supply the town with electricity as part of the deal! Douglas had been one of the first towns in the British Isles to have a public gas supply (1835) but it was to be one of the last to have a public electricity supply, which was not effected until 1923. There was irony in the fact that the borough's first electrical engineer came from the Manx Electric Railway (as it was known by then), where he had been the chief assistant.

Undaunted, in 1895 the tramway directors turned their attentions to building a tramway from Laxey to the top of Snaefell, the Island's highest mountain. Imagine trying to obtain planning permission for such a scheme now! And in the following year they built a cable tramway to serve upper Douglas, by now the new burgeoning capital.

At the same time another electric tramway was constructed by a different concern – the Douglas Southern Electric Tramway Ltd – along the route of the established Marine Drive. Running between Douglas and Port Soderick, a distance of three miles, it gave spectacular views of the coast south of the capital and was the only rail undertaking in the Island to use the standard British gauge of four feet eight and a half inches. It had a depot on a remote headland at Little Ness and a power station on an equally exposed headland at Pigeon Stream.

Incredibly, many of these transport systems survive. Not only can you still ride in the original electric cars and horsedrawn trams – you can also travel in railway carriages hauled by the Island's first steam locomotive, dating from 1873!

BOOM TOWNS

Victorian visitors revelled in these novelties and the Island prospered. It even survived the effects of the First World War and the depression of the mid 1920's. The other towns in the Island benefited from the boom and by 1880 Ramsey had a population of 4,000 and, seeing the opportunities for attracting tourism, laid out new promenades and streets. Sadly its full potential was never realised and the grand schemes for the promenades were never completed.

In the south of the Island, the small fishing villages of Port Erin and Port St Mary more than doubled in size with the coming of the railway. Boarding houses were built, though Port St Mary hung on to its traditional boatbuilding skills. In stark contrast nearby Castletown, having lost its long-held status as the Island capital to Douglas in 1863, ironically faced a period of decline, the ancient town receiving only a limited boost from the tourism business.

There were no such problems for Peel, on the west coast. Dominated by the castle on St Patrick's Isle, it was and still is a place of great charm and natural beauty that visitors quickly warm to. Moreover, it retained its position as the fishing capital of the Island, with 200 boats registered in the port in 1880 and more than 2,000 men employed in the industry. It became famous for its kipper processing, and even today in season Peel still carries the aroma of smoking herring.

The town was also well endowed with schools, in particular a mathematical school that specialised in navigation and produced many noteworthy sea captains.

CLINCHS

The Chequered Flag

With continued investment in the holiday industry and a great influx of visitors from the north-west of England, tourism outstripped agriculture as Mann's principal revenue earner and the Island enjoyed a period of boom.

Then came an invasion of another kind – one from which the Isle of Man has never recovered. The motor car arrived, and it didn't do so quietly. The reason was that the Automobile Club of Great Britain and Ireland (forerunner of the RAC) was looking for suitable venues to host the Gordon Bennett Cup Race, in which British cars had already enjoyed success on the continent. In 1903 the event was held in Ireland, but the following year it came to the Isle of Man for the eliminating trials, which involved racing motor cars on public roads.

The Governor of the Island at that time was Lord Raglan, who was sympathetic to the cause. A Road Races Act was promptly passed to accommodate both racing and the closure of public roads – a deed which changed the nature of tourism on the Island and is still very evident today. And not only did the Island support car racing; from 1907 it became host to the annual Tourist Trophy motorcycle races, famous throughout the world.

Being exposed to these 'new-fangled' machines also had an effect on the Island's own forms of transport, and it was not long before the horsedrawn trams and the railways were facing competition from motor charabancs and buses. By this time the Isle of Man Steam Packet Company was bringing somewhere in the order of 100,000 visitors a year to the Island. In addition, ships of the various railway companies were operating to Heysham and Fleetwood, swelling these numbers still higher and helping to create a greater need than ever for accommodation and entertainment.

The Castle Mona and the Fort Anne had already become hotels. In 1877 another private residence was acquired at Derby Castle and by 1884 a large dance hall had been built on the site. The Palace Ballroom quickly followed, occupying part of the former Castle Mona estate and commanding a central position on the promenade. It was the largest dance hall in the British Isles, just beating the Tower Ballroom at Blackpool to the honour. Next came several theatres in Douglas, which also boasted two iron piers – one at Broadway and the other at Derby Castle. Ramsey too soon had an iron pier, stretching almost half a mile into the bay, but it was purely functional. Subsequently named The Queen's Pier, it provided a low-water berthing for ships of the Isle of Man Steam Packet Company, who ran regular services from the port.

The charabanc (derived from the French char à bancs – literally a coach or carriage with benches) became synonymous with holidaymakers as a whole variety of exciting travel options was offered, from round-Island excursions to trips that took in all the principal towns, or the Island's picturesque glens, or places of entertainment such as Rushen Abbey. The Victorians delighted in such activities.

It was boom time. Everyone prospered with the new tourism industry: boarding houses were everywhere and holiday camps started to appear, in those days providing young men with cheap accommodation under canvas! 'Go abroad to the Isle of Man' was the holiday slogan of the day.

But even the Isle of Man could not escape the shattering effects of the 1914-18 war. All of the Island's able-bodied young men answered the call to arms, and an Alien Detention Camp was set up at Knockaloe, a farm in the west of the Island, to accommodate up to 20,000 prisoners of war. A two-mile branch line was built to connect the camp by railway to Peel. There were other military establishments on the Island, all serviced by the railway and the limited number of motor buses then available.

After the war the Island was quick to return to normality, and happy days were here again as people from the north-west of England were keen to 'get away from it all'. However, Islanders deeply felt the loss of the Steam Packet's flagship *Ben my Chree III* – one of eleven of the company's fleet of ships requisitioned for war service and one of four lost in action. She was the fastest conventional ship ever built for the Steam Packet, and the Manx were proud of her and 'their company' in a way that is hard to imagine today.

Apart from the adverse effects of the general strike of 1926, the number of visitors coming to the Isle of Man was soon surpassing the pre-war figures, which in 1913 had been in the region of 500,000. Cunningham's Young Men's Holiday Camp, used as an internment camp during the war, was back in business by 1919 and proved so popular that many tents were replaced by chalets and other more permanent facilities. These included a chair escalator running from Little Switzerland near the Queen's Promenade up to the camp on the top of the cliff.

This increased prosperity enjoyed by the Island led to more major civil engineering works, this time to improve the sewers in Douglas and to widen the Loch Promenade. The scheme also incorporated sunken gardens and a wide walkway. A new power station was built at Pulrose in 1929, but such was the demand for electricity that by 1936 it had to be extended. The promenade at Peel was widened and the breakwater improved to facilitate the berthing of Steam Packet vessels plying between Peel and Belfast.

Stan Basnett

Motorcycle racing on the **TT Course**

The prosperity of the Steam Packet Company was a further indicator of how well the Island was doing, and towards the end of the decade the company built three new ships for its Irish Sea routes. One of these vessels was *Lady of Mann*, launched in the company's centenary year and representing the ultimate in cross-channel steamers. In 1929 the ships of the Steam Packet carried more than a million passengers to and from the Island.

On the entertainment front it was the era of the cinema, and Douglas boasted five. The Crescent, in the centre of the promenade, was the largest, seating 2,000 people. To walk along the promenade was to run the gauntlet of the charabanc and landau touts as they vied to persuade holidaymakers to take a trip to the Point of Ayre, Glen Maye or Port Erin, or to Rushen Abbey for strawberries and cream, or to splash out on a round-the-Island or evening Mystery Tour.

An unexpected spin-off from the war was the sudden nationwide surplus of aircraft – machines which, technically speaking, had developed at a phenomenal rate. Pleasure flights became one of the crazes of the twenties, along with partying and dancing. A V Roe & Company, a name destined to become significant in the history of flight, obtained permission from Douglas Corporation to operate flights from the foreshore, and duly stationed two planes on the grass plot at Queen's Promenade. Complaints about noise soon put paid to these pleasure flights, but the opportunity was quickly seized to bring in the daily newspapers from England by air, ensuring that Islanders could buy them in the morning instead of waiting for their arrival by sea in the afternoon!

The Isle of Man was host to motor car racing again from 1933 to 1935 – a period when a

depression was being felt throughout Britain. The races were run around Douglas, starting and finishing on the promenade. The following two years saw the races move to a circuit on the outskirts of the town, which became known as the Parkfield Circuit, and in 1937 the winning driver was Prince Birabongse of Siam in an ERA.
Meanwhile the aeroplane did not go away. In fact, the Island attracted many famous aviators, all striving to create interest in establishing an airfield. Their persistence was rewarded in the shape of Ronaldsway, near Castletown, and in 1933 the Blackpool and West Coast Air Services became the first of many companies to operate to the Isle of Man. De Havilland Dragons and Rapides became a familiar sight, and before long a mail contract was won. Air transport had arrived.
In 1935, on land belonging to Close Lake Farm in the north of the Island, another airfield was opened. It stood on the site of the ancient Lake Mirescog and was named the Hall Caine Airport in memory of Sir Hall Caine, the famous Manx novelist, whose family raised the money for the venture. Services were operated to Liverpool, Blackpool, Belfast and Glasgow.

A NEW BEGINNING

In 1939 came the calamity that had been signalled for so long as Britain was once again drawn into conflict with Germany. Practically all of the hotels and boarding houses in the Island were requisitioned, surrounded with barbed wire fences and turned into internment camps. Those that weren't became military training establishments. Petrol rationing kept virtually all but military vehicles off the road. Buses operated within the towns and the Isle of Man Railway entered another period of intense working, carrying not only local people but also large numbers of internees and military personnel.
A Royal Air Force station, built from scratch on land at Jurby in 1938, opened in 1939 as a training establishment – a function it retained until 1964, when the Manx government took over ownership. During the war it also housed operational squadrons from time to time. In 1941 another RAF airfield was built at Andreas, also in the north of the Island, as a base for fighter squadrons.
Meanwhile, Island resources were once again requisitioned for military use. Ronaldsway was eventually commissioned as HMS Urley, a training establishment for Royal Naval air crews, and ships of the Isle of Man Steam Packet Company performed with distinction in Admiralty service, particularly at the evacuation of Dunkirk. By the end of the conflict the company had lost four vessels and the others that returned were in a generally poor state. The Steam Packet immediately initiated a fleet replacement programme, which saw five sister ships delivered between 1946 and 1955, starting with *King Orry IV* and ending with *Manxman II*. The company looked optimistically to a return to the bonanza of the pre-war years.
The clip clop of horses' hooves became a familiar sound again as the horse trams resumed service on the promenade; not for the visitors, but as transport for local people. The Corporation's Tilling-Stevens petrol electric buses, some of which dated from 1926, were worn out and overdue for replacement, and other public service vehicles were showing their age. This was a difficult time: the infrastructure of the Island was tired, men who had travelled to foreign parts during the war were unsettled, boarding houses needed repair for the 1946 season, and new buses were slow in coming because the rest of the British Isles had even greater problems and the Island had to take its turn.
The Manx people, resilient as ever, rose to the challenge, accepting that tourism was unlikely to return to its pre-war level. Nevertheless, there were still a significant number of visitors to the Island – about 400,000. Stars such as Joe Loss and Ivy Benson became synonymous with the Villa Marina, and the Palace attracted acts of the calibre of Cyril Stapleton, Ronnie Aldrich and the Squadronaires. And while agriculture replaced tourism as the number one industry, it was not all bad news.
Prince Birabongse was back sporting the national racing colours of Siam – blue racing overalls and blue ERA. The Island hosted the British Empire Trophy, a motor race competed on a version of the pre-war Parkfield Circuit. This car racing

Peel Castle – now an attractive venue for plays and concerts

was short lived but the motorcycling continued, the annual summer holiday season sandwiched between the TT and Manx Grand Prix events.

The seasonal fluctuations in visitor numbers became something of a problem; everyone did very nicely in summer but winter could be a desperate time. Islanders dependent on tourism faced a choice of the dole or participating in the winter works projects conceived by the insular government, or – even worse – leaving the Island to work in the sugarbeet industry.

During the fifties the population of the Isle of Man fell to just below 48,000 as young people left to seek employment elsewhere. Efforts to redress the balance saw the introduction of light industry to the Island, with some success as a short-term solution.

The government decided that the answer was to increase the population figure to a self-sustaining level and to replace the ailing tourism industry with something else that was labour intensive and not materials based. With this came the realisation that the Island might once again be able to capitalise on its advantageous tax regime. Once the die was cast there was no turning back. Overtures were made to the international finance sector and large financial institutions, who saw the benefits of becoming offshore in the Isle of Man. A target figure of 80,000 was set for the ideal population, and the touchpaper was lit.

The tourism industry stabilised at something like 300,000 visitors a year during the 1960's. By 1969, 200,000 were arriving by air. BEA was among several companies competing for business and air travel had improved beyond all recognition. Ronaldsway Airport was upgraded to receive the advanced new BAC 1-11 jet aircraft, operated by BEA on their London-Isle of Man-Belfast route.

Then came another blow to the tourism business – the advent of package holidays to foreign climes where sun was virtually guaranteed. The low-cost, all-inclusive prices simply couldn't be matched.

One answer was the introduction of car ferries on the Isle of Man routes, which helped bring in more visitors by sea. It also attracted competition in the seventies for the Steam Packet in the shape of a new rival, Manx Line.

This operated to Heysham and offered the first Ro-Ro (roll on, roll off) service. The Steam Packet responded with a like service.

In 1973 Britain joined the European Community but the Isle of Man remained outside and is still not a full member. However, through Protocol 3 of the Treaty of Accession the Manx Government has retained freedom of trade between the Isle of Man and EU countries.

By 1976 the Island's population had grown to 60,500. Clearly, the policy formulated in earlier years was working The gradual arrival of reputable financial organisations was attracting others in the same line of business, providing the necessary stimulus for the growth of a more stable economy.

Improvements long overdue were carried out to Douglas harbour, with a new breakwater and comprehensive Ro-Ro facilities and marshalling areas. The Isle of Man Steam Packet Company acquired up-to-date freight and passenger ships, including some of the world's latest fastcraft. Ronaldsway Airport was further upgraded to equip it for the standard of service demanded by modern business customers, and today Manx Airlines faces healthy competition from a number of rivals, though it remains the principal operator with daily services to several major UK cities.

In 1979 the Isle of Man celebrated the Millennium of Tynwald – the system of self-government introduced by Norse settlers and still in use today. The year was marked with special events and the number of visitors for the season topped the 400,000 mark – the first time since the immediate post-war years.

By the early eighties the Island was firmly established as a progressive offshore insurance centre, and to keep pace with its development further legislation and other measures were introduced. These included stringent regulatory controls and the establishment of a Financial Supervision Commission. At the same time the Isle of Man Shipping Register, in existence since 1786, was seen as another way of promoting economic growth and employment, and the means was created to extend the register worldwide and ensure it complied with the latest maritime legislation. The Isle of Man became a full Maritime Convention country, guaranteeing a standard of excellence and putting itself firmly on the map. Now more than twenty ship management companies operate

from the Island and there are 235 ships on the Isle of Man Register.

As with any island economy, the difficult task for government has been to strike the delicate balance between retaining the way of life cherished for so long while meeting the demands of modern business.

There have been many impacts on the Island during this latest period of evolution. For example, in 1960 there were 2,000 vehicles registered in the Island – now there are 53,000! In 1991 the population had grown to 69,788, and the construction industry remains buoyant as the

demand for housing and new office accommodation grows with the gradual renewal of the old Victorian infrastructure. And the new, bigger power stations at Pulrose and Peel are generating the electricity to satisfy the Island's new businesses.

The finance sector is now Mann's main employer and makes the largest contribution to the economy. Industry is second and tourism, though fourth in this economic league table, is still playing a very important role. By focusing on specialised holidays such as sporting events, and making potential visitors more aware of the Island's unique history, heritage, culture, natural beauty and remarkable transport systems, the Isle of Man is succeeding in attracting new admirers from all over the world.

And for the Manx people themselves, the most significant impact of this exciting new chapter in the Island's history has been a period of full employment. The opportunities available to young people and school leavers have never looked more enticing, and the need to leave the Island to find work and a career is a diminishing trend. The goal has almost been reached – and the spirit of Mann lives on.

The afternoon train at **Ballabeg** – the smallest station on the **Steam Railway**

An extract from

BETSY LEE

"Now the beauty of the thing when childher plays is
The terrible wonderful length the days is.
Up you jumps, and out in the sun,
And you fancy the day will never be done;
And you're chasin' the bumbees hummin' so cross
In the hot sweet air among the goss,
Or gath'rin' blue-bells, or lookin' for eggs,
Or peltin' the ducks with their yalla legs,
Or a climbin' and nearly breakin' your skulls,
Or a shoutin' for divilment after the gulls,
Or a thinkin' of nothin', but down at the tide
Singin' out for the happy you feel inside.
That's the way with the kids, you know,
And the years do come and the years do go,
And when you look back it's all like a puff,
Happy and over and short enough."

by T E Brown

The changing face of **Douglas**

New office building – helping to equip **Douglas** for the next millennium

The changing face of **Douglas** with the new **HSBC** premises *(right)* harmonising with the Italianate facade of the **Isle of Man Bank** *(above)*

The beautiful glass dome in the banking
hall of the **Isle of Man Bank's Head Office**

The lights of Douglas Bay

Douglas at night – with the recently refurbished **Falcon Cliff** *(left)* and the new offices for the **Midocean Group** on the site of the former **Fort Anne Hotel** *(above)*

Government Buildings, Douglas

Unique **Isle of Man Post Office** stamps

Local currency issued by the **Isle of Man Treasury**

The new courthouse in **Douglas**

Left
Herring sculpture hanging in the foyer of the courthouse

An extract from the
OATH OF DEEMSTER
"... I do swear that I will without respect of favour or friendship, love or gain, consanguinity or affinity, envy or malice, execute the Laws of this Isle justly, betwixt our Sovereign LADY THE QUEEN and Her subjects within this Isle and betwixt Party and Party as indifferently as the Herring backbone doth lie in the midst of the Fish."

Far left
Tynwald Chambers

Previous pages
Inside the **House of Keys**

MARKS
&
SPENCER
DRUMGOLD STREET
CAR PARK

The main shopping area of **Douglas**

The magnificent
Gaiety Theatre

Douglas and surrounding hills

A peaceful moment in
Braddan Old Churchyard

Ben my Chree in **Douglas harbour**

New walkway at the sea terminal in **Douglas**

Right The view of **Douglas** from **Onchan Head**

 Sunset over **Douglas Bay**

Stan Basnett

The spectacular **TT Motorcycle Race Festival** held in June each year

HONDA

YAMAHA
DATA CENTRE
WEATHER REPORT
DAMP PATCHES
AT

41
MANX ELECTRIC RAILWAY

Stan Basnett

The charming **Groudle Glen narrow gauge railway** run by enthusiasts

Stan Basnett

Springtime in **Molly Quirk's Glen**

The **Manx Electric Railway** at **Lhen Coan**

The viaduct, built in 1894, carries the road and tramway over **Groudle Glen**

Groudle Glen waterfall

Groudle Glen – peace and tranquillity

The Great Wheel at **Laxey** – completed in 1854 to pump water from the lower levels of the mine workings

The wheel is the largest surviving waterwheel in the world, with a diameter of 22 metres

Opposite page
Laxey harbour

KONDOR
TERIFA
DO9

Laxey Station on the **Manx Electric Railway** – a mecca for rail enthusiasts

Special events are now commonplace: 1998 saw the celebration of **125 years of steam railways** on the Island

Stan Basnett

Right
View over **Laxey** from **Ballaragh**

Next page
The tramway in its dramatic location above **Bulgham Bay**

45
MANX ELECTRIC RAILWAY.
THE MANX ELECT

AILWAY Co.LTD.

Ballaglass Glen

The spectacular **Dhoon Glen** waterfall

An ancient **Celtic cross** in
Maughold Churchyard

Stan Basnett

Maughold Church
with **North Barrule**
in the distance

Looking across **Port Mooar** towards
Maughold Head

Right
View south from **Maughold Head**

Next page
The first rays of dawn over **Maughold Head**

Yn Chruinnaght festival held in Ramsey each year

Mooragh Park, Ramsey

Ramsey harbour

Yn Chruinnaght

The **Point of Ayre lighthouse** – built in 1818 at the most northerly point of the Island

Bride Church

The sand cliffs of the **north west coast**

The old parish church of **St Mary** de **Ballaugh**

Tholt y Will from **Bloc Eary**

Opposite page
Sulby Valley

A view across the **northern plain**

Jurby Church

Left
Sulby River and the upper reaches of **Sulby Glen**

Sulby Reservoir

The **Snaefell Mountain Railway**

An **electric tramcar** on the western slopes of **Snaefell**

The **Laxey Terminus**

Centenary celebrations with steam power on the **Snaefell Mountain Railway**

Arrival at the summit

Kirk Michael Parish Church

The waterfall at **Spooyt Vane**

The **Baldwins**

Injebreck at the head of the **West Baldwin Valley**

Winter's mantle **Injebreck**

RS

Carraghan mountain dominates the reservoir

Dinghy racing on the reservoir at **Injebreck**

Scenes from the annual **Tynwald Day Ceremony** held on 5th July

After the formal ceremony the fair is the major attraction, with stalls and displays throughout the day

Glen Helen – another of the Island's seventeen national glens

Rhenass Falls at **Glen Helen**

Opposite page
The west coast looking towards **White Strand** from **Peel** headlands

Following page
Peel Castle and the ancient cathedral of **St German** with the sandstone cliffs of the west coast in the background

Peel harbour with the elegant light on the breakwater and the very typical 'pepper pot' light on the jetty

Peel – home of the kipper and modern-day 'Vikings'

Left
A corner of old **Peel**

Peel Castle on a winter's day

... and cold work in the harbour

PL22

Sunset off the west coast

Fishing at **Peel** breakwater

View of **Peel** across the harbour and **Fenella beach**

Stan Basnett

A wintery evening near **Fleshwick**

Glen Maye waterfall

Niarbyl

Port Erin – the lower promenade from **Traie Meanagh**

Bradda Head and the old mine workings

Sunset from the top of **Bradda Head**
and the
promenade at **Port Erin**

The **Chicken Rock** lighthouse built in 1875

The Burroo – a small islet off the **Calf of Man**

Opposite page
Sugar Loaf Rock – known in Manx as **Cashtal Kione ny Goagyn**

Anvil Rock at **Kione ny Goagyn** near **Port St Mary**

Sugar Loaf Rock from the sea

Cregneash in the south of the Island was the first 'open-air' folk museum in the British Isles

Most of the village and farm is owned by **Manx National Heritage** and demonstrations of the old way of life...

... such as ploughing, weaving and spinning ...

... are carried out throughout the summer season

Opposite page
Mist lingers in the **Sound** between the **Island** and the **Calf of Man**

23
UNION

Port St Mary – the yachtsman's haven

The Sound and **Thousla Rock**

"Tally ho!"

Castletown and **Castle Rushen**

The harbour at Castletown

Castletown – the Island's ancient capital until the 1860s

Castletown harbour

Castletown still retains its charm and character

Agriculture is still an important part of the Island's economy

The **agricultural shows** bring the farmer to the public

Sheep farming is the main agricultural activity

Loaghtan Sheep – the traditional **Manx breed**

The tranquillity that is
Derbyhaven

Herring Tower on
Langness Peninsula

Opposite page
Castletown Golf Links Hotel
on **Langness**

View of **Langness Peninsula**

Ronaldsway Airport – providing modern facilities for the operators who connect the Island to destinations throughout the British Isles

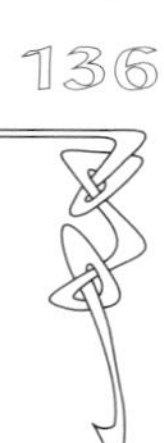

manx

G-MANA
G-MANM

manx
skianyn vannin
TUG 6

Sunset over **South Barrule**

Cass ny Hawin (the foot of the river) where **Santon Gorge** meets the sea

Isle of Man Steam Railway
– the ideal way to see the countryside –

seen here climbing out of **Douglas**

and at **Ronaldsway Halt** for the airport

The **Marine Drive** with views of the east coast from **Little Ness** and **Wallberry**

Dawn over **Douglas** and the harbour with its modern Ro-Ro facilities

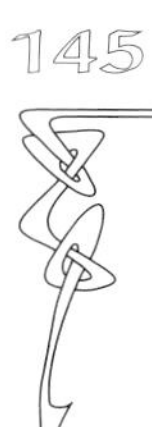

The **Tower of Refuge** at sunrise

Dawn over **Maughold Head**

Ellan Vannin

When the summer day is over and its busy cares have flown,
I sit beneath the starlight with a weary heart alone:
Then rises like a vision sparkling bright in nature's glee,
My own dear Ellan Vannin with its green hills by the sea.

Then I hear the wavelets murmur as they kiss the fairy shore;
Then beneath the em'rald waters sings the mermaid as of yore,
And the fair isle shines with beauty as in youth it dawn'd on me,
My own dear Ellan Vannin with its green hills by the sea.

Then Mem'ries sweet and tender come like music's plaintive flow,
Of the hearts in Ellan Vannin that loved me long ago;
And I give with tears and blessings, my fondest thought to thee,
My own dear Ellan Vannin with its green hills by the sea.

Lyrics by Eliza Craven Green